For

*Wishing you joy,
vision, amazement!*

*Blessings,
Diane*

ENTERING
THE
WORD TEMPLE

POEMS BY
DIANE FRANK

BLUE LIGHT PRESS ◆ 1ST WORLD LIBRARY

AUSTIN ◆ FAIRFIELD ◆ DELHI

Entering the Word Temple

1ST WORLD LIBRARY
PO Box 2211, Fairfield, Iowa 52556
www.1stworldlibrary.com

BLUE LIGHT PRESS
PO Box 642, Fairfield, Iowa 52556

BOOK DESIGN & INTERIOR ART:
Melanie Gendron

COVER ART:
"Entering the Mandala" by Philip Sugden

PHOTOGRAPH:
Anders Hansen

Entering the Word Temple website:
www.dianefrank.net

FIRST EDITION
Library of Congress Catalog Card Number: 2005908257
ISBN: 1-59540-905-X

ACKNOWLEDGMENTS

Grateful acknowledgment is made to the following magazines and anthologies in which some of these poems were previously published or accepted for publication:

The Briar Cliff Review, The Haight Ashbury Literary Journal, The Contemporary Review, Carquinez Poetry Review, *Convergence, The Dryland Fish, Eunoia, Fact of the Universe, Encore, River of Earth and Sky – Poems for the Twenty-First Century, Passive Fists: An Anthology by Poets for Peace*, and *After the Baby's Birth: A Woman's Way to Wellness* by Robin Lim.

"Orchid Backlit in Saturated Light" received the First Place Massachusetts State Poetry Society Award in the NFSPS 2003 competition.

Special thanks to Rustin Larson, David Hurlin, Robin Lim, Melanie Gendron, Rodney Charles, Suzanne Niedermeyer and the Monday Night Poets.

CONTENTS

Visions from the Right Hand of the Madonna

Orchid Backlit in Saturated Light..................................1
My Mother's Daughter..................................3
Visions from the Right Hand of the Madonna.............5
Walking over the Bridge..................................8
Venus of the Birds..................................11
Autumn in Iowa..................................14
Linda Street..................................15
Nadi Leaves..................................19

Entering the Word Temple

Every Monday I Put Herbs in his Water Bottle............26
Meridians..................................28
Botticelli's Angels..................................32
Virgins in the Uffizi..................................34
Venetian Blinds..................................37
Entering the Word Temple..................................40
Ascending..................................45
Requiem for a Pond..................................47
Fourth of July in Fairfield, Iowa..................................50
They Thought it was a Dragon Kite..................................51

Chagall in the City of Angels

What my Betta Fish is Dreaming..................................54
After She Fell from the Summit of the Body Sculpture..56
Belly Dance..................................59
Tsunami..................................61
The Goddess of Midnight..................................63
Chagall in the City of Angels..................................70
Market Street Angel..................................72
Lessons in Astronomy..................................75

Hiking by the Hudson River..78
When Their Love Leaks through the Ceiling..............80
Pouring Sand..83

Woman with a Green Donkey

Bees...88
Two Rivers...90
River of Light..94
Bells of Brunate..97
Woman with a Green Donkey....................................98
Batik Goddesses..99
Turtle Woman...101
Invitation to the Labyrinth.......................................102
Slices of Papaya...104
The Apocalypso Tantric Boys Choir.........................106
Ambivalence Souffle..108

Mask Awakening Egyptian Dream

Tennis Ballet...112
Late Afternoon in the Wakodahatchie Wetlands........116
Inside a Profusion of Birds.......................................118
Main Street in Cedar Falls...120
Autumn is Bare Chested..122
Prayer for Lydia and David.......................................123
Gypsy Round...124
In the Italian Ghetto..126
Deja Vu..128
Translation...129
What My Father Taught Me......................................131
Finding You...133
Mask Awakening Egyptian Dream...........................134

About the Author...138
About the Artists...139

ENTERING
THE
WORD
TEMPLE

VISIONS FROM
THE RIGHT HAND
OF THE MADONNA

ORCHID BACKLIT IN SATURATED LIGHT

The photograph I most wanted was blurred. Hands were placed on his head in a gesture of blessing, but his face was out of focus. My emotions were swirling between the Sahara Desert and the South Pole, with a magnetic shift oscillating in the ionosphere.

He shows up to dance with broken angel wings, searching below seven shields of beauty for a familiar face. We spend the week sewing costumes – silk, velvet, lilac flowers on shaded backgrounds – to move ourselves backward through time. In the late afternoon, we stitch ourselves into Renaissance and Elizabethan ballrooms. We connect our fingers across the rose satin of American Prairie ballgowns and Romeo shirts. Then we roll sushi for dinner.

It's confusing when you dance – eye to eye, so close. As your hands connect, you feel the trajectory of the circle you move through leaning back into time. You feel like you've danced this way for thousands of years with the same eyes in different bodies. Suddenly, you're in love. For a moment, the colors and countries bleed through tinted leaves. Twigs of rhododen-dron forests break under your bare feet, but it doesn't mean you have a future.

The angels say sleep on the ground so you can feel the wetness of alfalfa fields below your heart. Let the moisture in the earth seep into the quilt you've been stitching for seven years. Even though the moon is a sliver now, it will send its silver light into your dreams. They keep the future hidden so you can learn, but the guidance comes from inside, like a melody you heard from the flowers when you were three years old but forgot to tell anyone.

A group of traveling musicians says there is a tree in India with the pattern of everyone's life printed on the leaves. The flute player said it was in a courtyard on the way to Shangri-La. You know the place by the silk draped over the Goddess with six arms. You can visit her there, in the scented garden of her secret flowers, or wait for a message in a dream. She is a wild orchid flying across the moon, and what you have forgotten is drowning.

Sometimes when I look at photographs, I feel like I'm looking at ghosts — people who have disappeared into other lives. Sometimes when I look into the mirror, my face is far away, but there are footsteps between the tiger lilies behind the empty lot at the corner. The music in the mud under the orchids is pulling me to the earth, planting roots there. I am the woman under the veil. This is what I am dreaming.

MY MOTHER'S DAUGHTER

It is five years before I was born,
before life ruined her.

She is already sixteen years old,
breasts rising like yeasted bread
which she tries to conceal on the streets
of her immigrant neighborhood,
but when she sings with Tommy Dorsey's Big Band,
she stuffs her dress with tissues,
paints her lips red,
and styles her hair like Judy Garland.

At Weequahic High School
she joins the hall patrol
to station herself outside the door
of my father's sixth period class.
She's smiling every afternoon
when he walks out of the door.

Later they escape to the West Village
in his red convertible
to the apartment he shares with his half brother
in a loft filled with etchings.

When he walks into the night club
where she pretends to be eighteen years old,
she sings to my father
directly with bedroom eyes,
How High the Moon
blasting out of Tommy's trombone
and then cascading from her mouth.
Who could resist such a song?

By the subway stop to Harlem
to see Billie Holiday,
he buys two gardenias for her hair.
A few months later,
they hitchhike to a cabin
by Caroga Lake in upstate New York,
share a bottle of wine,
throw the glasses into the fire
and create me.

Years later, my mother will tell me how
I ruined her career,
but she has a transparent face.
In the photograph
in the small apartment in Spanish Harlem
where they lived after I was born,
I see her completely happy.

VISIONS FROM THE RIGHT HAND
OF THE MADONNA

1.

She brought me fresh baked bread
with rye flour, walnuts and onions
still warm from the oven.
In the heat I could feel her love.

It's been difficult to eat
but the bread says
look to the future.

It's in the scent of the onions
and the wheat. Inside
the skin of the tangerines
in the basket by my window.

2.

I dream about a man with angel hands
who touches with such ethereal tenderness
that it almost doesn't belong to this place.
He seems to be far away
from the pain of this planet.

The oil he massages into
my back and shoulders
is scented with lilacs.
I can feel love pouring out
from his fingertips,
but even the love seems to be
from somewhere else.

His hands spread visions across my skin
at the base of my spine
where hummingbirds build their nests.

Further north, a music
of breaking icicles
falls while the snow bear
walks through the moon.

On the other side of the tunnel
the aurora is turquoise
with polar bears walking
on the ice floe.

A river of turquoise light
is flowing through my body.
I don't know if he is an angel
or a Tantric magician,
but the roof is gone now.

The moon is a white lantern
in Kyoto
above the geisha district of Gion.

In the sake light
that floats between the bare branches
of plum trees,
I am walking down narrow alleys
towards the teahouse.

3.

In the alley beside my house
I burn letters
in three different languages.

Across the continent
two towers are falling
near the place of my birth.
In the minds of the people who live there
they fall again and again.

But on the altar
in front of the church
that is home for the rescue workers,
people from all places
bring poems, sculpture, photographs,
a bronze dancing Shiva inside a circle of flowers,
Indonesian finger puppets, tribal masks from Africa,
blue and yellow banners from firemen,
the Black Madonna, yellow roses,
uniforms from policemen,
crayon posters from school children,
Our Lady of Guadalupe
and an ancient Hebrew blessing.

Every morning the women
bring new roses
even though three months later
the ground is still smoking.
The memory falls in
smoke so thick you can't
see out to your hand,
a banner painted by school children
draped over the fence
at the edge of the graveyard.

But somewhere else,
three degrees to the right of feminine,
an angel rides a green donkey
to the moon, tossing flowers
to the aurora.

Walking Over the Bridge

For Don and Janis Langstaff

Her face was like an egg
but glowing. Around her,
lilacs from the gardens
of her friends.
Hair gone from chemotherapy.
She chanted names of the friends
who surrounded her
in those final moments.
You look so lovely in lavender
today. Like a lilac. I love you!
So good of you to come.
I love you! I love you!
When we come to the place
where she asked us to gather
inside a grove of old trees,
the chanting comes from the leaves.

He walks a white gravel path
in the dark, listening
for the bass vibrato of tree frogs
by the reservoir.
They are silent when he stops
but sing when he moves again.
He walks under an arc of
elderberry trees
even though his night vision is blurred.
On a new wooden bridge
over the creek that leads to the North Pond,
he leans back against the railing
to see the way

branches cut the shape of the sky.
Old souls up there
inside of those flying stars.

The woman who sings to tree frogs
stopped throwing clay
after her mother died.
She smiles like a ten year old
when she says, *"I'm not a potter."*
She spreads her history of pots
on the lawn, in front of the
yard sale sign,
surrounds them with elderberry blossoms
for white deer to eat.
Before the sun sets
my house is filled with pots she made.
The lily vase, the olive pot,
a globe with an entrance for wildflowers,
stacking bowls with gingko leaves
etched into the glaze,
the brown earth pot,
the blue sky pot.

In the house alone, I arrange
Winter Density lettuce,
slice tomatoes, peel cucumbers,
toss basil and dill weed from my garden
over glazed gingko leaves.
Still, there is a restlessness.
In another world
the singing of a cello
and a man who speaks as though he knows me
from the place where his own music
begins to breathe.

He reads my heart line,
says it arches up to the spirit,
to Pleiades, undiscovered stars.
Waiting for a vision,
I dream of leaf-shaped shadows,
dream of Saturn through a telescope,
dream of doors.

Walking into the dark,
or is that what they call the future,
I don't know my name anymore.
I am fragmented, disintegrated,
lost between the images of my dreams.
I am seven women
looking for a copper bowl
or a voice, the Milky Way
in a sugar scoop.
But I can walk this way
for miles at night sometimes
with Pleiades trickling its ancient sugar light
across a distance too large
to be imagined.
There are times when
the tension between who I am
and who I long to be
pulls me over the bridge,
Brahma cow licking at my elbow.

Venus of the Birds

She disappeared on a Thursday
in the evening with a stranger
and a dream of Monarch butterflies,
leaving the bare wood floors
for Wisconsin or California.
She didn't leave a message
or a note for her friends –
only shampoo and a bicycle
in the middle of an empty room.
Only the echo of Chinese vases,
bottles of herbs,
and two Tibetan bells.

When she swam in *Lago di Como,*
boats turned. The fishermen
came closer to see
the young woman swimming
toward the island in a white bikini
while fish flapped in wooden buckets.
When she kneeled in churches,
statues spoke to her.
In the late afternoon
she walked in the *piazza*
weaving between the restless crowds
of young Italian men.
One of them wanted her to go with him,
but she couldn't speak the language.
She didn't know how to say
yes, or no.

In the afternoons she rode her bicycle
into the fields, searching for wildflowers,
a perfect lavender calyx,
a field of tiger lilies
with tangerine four o'clock light
shining through the petals.
She wanted to learn the language of birds,
the chant of the meadowlark,
the blue arc of the barn swallow,
Canada geese flying home.

She always felt like a stranger,
even in her dreams.
At midnight she cocoons herself
inside a circle of candles,
tones with Tibetan bells
to invent a new language.
In her garden she plants
watermelon, comfrey and zucchini,
her melon breasts swimming at the edge
of her white muslin blouse.

She stops eating, except for herbs
and juice from the vegetables
she grows in her garden,
but her father won't disappear,
especially in the dreams
where she harvests lightning.
She has to go away.
By her window
a tangerine sweater tossed over a chair,
blackberry vines stretching
to a sliver moon.

Her friends search their dreams for visions,
ask for messages from the birds.
Outside, behind the barn
a cluster of black-eyed Susans.
A hummingbird hovers, flies low,
but escapes my hand.
Perhaps she has become a butterfly.
I hope she is in Wisconsin
or California
face lifted to the sky, her voice a breeze
through the petals of sunflowers.
I can almost see her
sleepwalking through an empty room
with a painted flute,
searching for her own music
to whisper to the birds.

AUTUMN IN IOWA

I stuff *I Ching* pennies
into a parking meter.
The sun tilts through colored glass,
turns blue in my kitchen window.

We put on costumes for Halloween.
I dance after midnight
with a bare-chested man
with boxing gloves.

The peony stalks are brittle
in the wind, and the coneflowers
have turned brown before November.
Field mice bury their fur
inside the quiet places of the heart.

LINDA STREET

"Light leaves no footprints on the sky.
It knows how to vanish
and therefore remains forever."
Rabindranath Tagore

1. *Light leaves no footprints on the sky.*

I walk across the snowy field
crossing deer tracks,
open the log door to Brianna's cabin,
open windows to sunlight,
water ficus, pyrocantha, eucalyptus,
bamboo in Hong Kong glass,
crumple flowers
at the feet of saints,
cut up winter squash,
make soup,
sit in the sunny bay window seat.

My back against wood
sun on my face
makes me feel like I'm back in San Francisco
in the Mission District
looking down wooden stairways
and slanted roofs
from the bay window,
eight birds of paradise
drooping out of lavender glass
at Shana's house on Linda Street.

Over ramen with long beans and red snapper,
Shana's story about the man

15

she drove to Port Townsend
and how he totally lost it
while Robert Bly was reading shaman poetry
and pushing too hard for young poets
without any ego strength.
The man left her for a woman
who wasn't as pretty or smart
and wrote poetry that in a word sucked,
but was not competitive.
Shana decided to go to bed with women
for the next two years, and an occasional
gay man before the AIDS epidemic.

2. *It knows how to vanish...*

I went to Linda Street every Tuesday night,
walked up four flights of stairs
past *placas* and Latino
teenage lovers spooning on the stairs.
To park on Linda Street
or any place close to there,
you'd have to invoke the Parking Goddess
and then get lucky.

Maybe it's twenty years ago,
but Shana is talking to me
about the five things in her closet
she wears all the time.
She wants to get rid of the rest.
I'm wanting to get rid of my husband
climbing into my bed
smelling like sex from who knows where.
Shana is telling me
that when you're happy to wake up

16

somewhere else,
you're starting to get over it.

Right now the only thing I know
is the quality of light
on red tile roofs in the Mission District
at six o'clock in the morning
through the breaking fog,
lavender sheets like crumpled flowers.

3. *And therefore remains forever.*

I remember the first time
someone told me about spooning,
explained it like a can of sardines
but two people like sardines
in a canoe or a twin bed.

Stevie and I went to Jabberwocky Café
to hear James Taylor before he was famous.
He had a song on the radio now,
Fire and Rain,
but was still playing to crowds of eighty people
clustered around dayglow tables,
spooning on mats,
or hunched up on sitting blocks.

Stevie and I were leaning together
on a rectangle painted black,
legs dangling over a dayglow watermelon
the color of a sunset
just before the light leaves.

After the concert, we climbed the scaffold
up to the roof of a building being constructed
and read crumpled pieces of paper...
Lavender poems. "Colours" by Yevtushenko.
We didn't spoon because I was still a virgin
and an invisible rose-tinted angel
wanted me to preserve
a petal in my skin.

Stevie brought his sketch pad
inside the green house.
With a charcoal pencil, he drew me
under huge marijuana plants and yucca trees,
inside drug-warped mandalas
of gold around lavender and green.
He talked to me about how lines
expand and wander into shadows,
the black wrought iron of street lamps,
steel girders, wood and climbing.

It was the year of the daisy-painted minivan,
music that turned all night,
and leaves that turned into butterflies
at six o'clock in the morning.
Elbows became construction scaffolds
and knees straddled midnight fences,
an invitation to start climbing.
It was a time that nobody
could look at their own face.
Stevie was trying to paint his way out
of a boundary he could not transcend
until he disappeared one evening
without a footprint of light.

NADI LEAVES

"What is to give light
must endure burning."
Victor Frankel

1.

He sits in the Shiva Temple
about to sing, about to cry
crossing his left leg
into full lotus.

He is the youngest son of the Maharajah.
His parents build temples to Shiva,
but he desires children.

He marries a temple dancer,
her kathak red smile
a rising moon.
He wraps her in saris the color of
summer flowers.

Each time before he loves her,
he paints henna on her feet,
her hair long and dark,
a midnight waterfall.

But she is covered with veils,
especially in the womb.

2.

In his mother's house,
his second wife
cooks, cleans and loves him,
but every month
when the full moon rises
over the Shiva temple,
her blood comes.

He dreams of honey locust
long pods, huge thorns,
oleander, pink and red,
deadly poisonous.

He is painting his way out
of an egg that is
cracking.

A horizontal landscape
where you give into it —
an arm, a back, or a leg
and the body that transports you.

His wife dances like a goddess,
her womb
a shower of comets,
their trails blazing across
an inner sky.

The gods say,
"What is to give light
must endure burning."

3.

His third wife is young
and beautiful as the lilies
around the Shiva Temple.
She dances for him
with bells on silver anklets.

She follows him up the mountain
where he loves her,
shapes her like sculpture
under his hands.

In the Kali Gandaki River, the moon
floats, stretches and ripples,
becomes silver apples
dissolving,
spreading and gathering.

The snow falls for two winters
with the promise of children
who get lost in the caves
between the worlds.

Now he is wandering all over India.
His skin is bathed in ashes.
She is washing copper pots
in his mother's house.

In the Himalayas
under an avalanche of snow
he stops breathing.

4.

Under a Nadi tree
the priests at the Shiva Temple
write stories of the souls
who will later
find them.

Above them,
three women collide
in the belt of a constellation.
They engrave the messages
on Nadi leaves.

Five thousand years later
a saint who reads palm leaves
half way around the world
tells him the story.

He sends him back to India
to be passed under the
belly of a Brahma cow.

He travels to Bombay
with a woman who
holds a cello instead of a man
between her knees.

Her voice is a white deer,
the first opening
of a blossom.

She will wear a silver necklace
engraved with a *yantra*
and tiny stones in the colors
of the planets.

Every morning he brings
roses to her pillow.
She tells him
we are the stories
we invent.

ENTERING
THE WORD TEMPLE

EVERY MONDAY I PUT HERBS
IN HIS WATER BOTTLE

His grandfather is a Yemenite herbal doctor. He is an astronomer or a satellite engineer, but he is obsessed with herbs. I am an herbal shaman, and I always dance with herbs in my water bottle. If he asks me, I tell him the formula. Sometimes we dance together, when his wife or his dance partner doesn't come. A dance partner is like a wife in these circles and you can't interfere.

Sometimes we dance together, old couple dances like *Rachel* and *Shnei Shoshanim*. Usually his dance partner pulls him away from me. On nights when she is unbearable, I stand next to him in line for dances like *Debka Inbar* and *Al Salsalim*. I have to touch him, even if it's just his hand.

There's something unbearably sexy about muscular men who dance. Israelis have endorphins in their muscles – it's from their time in the army. The studio where I don't live anymore has the scent of a paratrooper who used to do push-ups with me curled around his back. Easier, he said, than a soldier on his back with a heavy pack on. The memory has molecules of endorphins.

American men on the dance floor can look at you in a way that you know they'd like to go to bed with you. Israeli men look at you like they're already in bed with you. Even when I'm standing next to him in line, he looks at me that way. His skin speaks to me in the language of an olive tree. His voice is my history.

When my desire is too strong to be appropriate, I dance with other men. But I know exactly where he is on the dance floor. At the end of the evening, I put aphrodisiac herbs in his water bottle and say, "This is for your wife."

He says, "What are you doing to me? You have no mercy. I won't be able to walk tomorrow." His skin is the same color as the paratrooper. They know the same form of deadly martial arts.

On the way home I listen to *Debka Inbar*. I play it over and over. By now he is in bed with his wife, but his eyes have no mercy. The music is inside me and reminds me of his skin.

MERIDIANS

Love is not an emotion.
Love is who you are.

1.

His hands told her
that he was one of the Tantric sculptors
of the Temple in Varanasi
where Hindu gods and goddesses
are perpetually making love.

Halfway around the world,
he traces the fire meridian
up her left leg.

The butterfly angel who dances
out of her heart chakra
has flame blue swallowtail
wings.

2.

Men are the sea she swims in.
In the Temple in Varanasi
or on the basketball floor of the gym
at the 43rd and Judah
Contra dance
in San Francisco.

She walks through the door
with a red pashmina shawl
draped around her shoulders.

Men are the sea she swims in
under floating summer light
when she dances
face to open face
with her eyes burning
a soft trail of fire.

He says,
"Let me be a soft cocoon
for you." He takes
her spinning through
soft blue light. He would
like to know the mystery.

During the silent prayer
she envisions his face —
blue pearl eyes,
the wide arc of his mouth,
his compassionate
face.

3.

She holds the sheets to her skin
wraps herself inside them
so she can breathe his molecules again.

An echo of burgundy satin
in the shape of the
ballgown she wore,

a single violet
fooled by November's warmth
into blooming,

the room where they danced
now empty except for
the echo of a flute.

4.

The location is nowhere,
something exotic, foreign
something more musical than linguistic.

His hands emerge
from inside a sculpture of lovers
he carved centuries ago,
beauty without a filter.

Half way around the world
the sky is clear night after night,
Pegasus and the Pleiades
floating above
a long arc of milky stars.

The sky is open, transparent
except for the evening
of the Leonid meteor showers
and his voice
outside her window.

At four o'clock in the morning,
he is singing, "Wake up! Shine!
Come with me and see
the stars flying across the sky!
Sing to me! Don't be afraid."

5.

She dreams she is a hummingbird
and she needs to fly
in the morning.

Her voice sings inside the sculpture
of the Temple at Varanasi,
beauty without a filter.

When she dances,
she discovers something about herself,
silver bells
wrapped around her ankles,
and the music comes from everywhere.

In another world
the contralto singing of a tamboura
and hands that teach her more deeply
who she is and where
she is located
on the Earth meridian.

Every time he speaks
a hummingbird
flies out of his mouth

And you have to
walk through fire
to go anywhere in her house.

BOTTICELLI'S ANGELS

The light is always a surprise.
You'll see an angel in the garden
surrounded by rhododendron leaves,
or on top of a fountain
you discover through the grating
in the courtyard of a Florentine church
surrounded by medieval walls.

An angel will surprise you
in flowers of the frescoes,
in the swirling blue translucence
of a long window of Venetian glass.
She'll wave at you under silk scarves
of olive skinned women with high cheekbones
and ripple in the laughter
of an old woman selling oranges.

In the *Duomo* angels wait for you
in the paint of Botticelli's garden,
in the light that surrounds the marble
of a lion with wings.
Above the Roman columns
angels hold up the carved ceiling.
They whisper from the light
inside flowers growing out
of the stone walls.

When you least expect it,
an angel offers you papaya
on a terra cotta plate.
Her head will appear in the bud

at the center of the rose
a stranger offers you in Venice.
At night she lights a soft
row of candles beside your bed.
When you dream, she covers you
in a rain of rose petals,
the pink of the wall as soft
as the blush on an angel's face.

Angels laugh at you
from a pirouette
on top of the vanilla
at the *Boffa Gelateria.*
They laugh as they connect the hands
of all of the lovers in Italy,
the country of love,
where all the flowers are glazed
with an aphrodisiac.

They weave invisible nets
between the fingers of the stranded.
When you least expect it,
a cloud shaped like an angel
will move away from the full moon.
The night is full of love and angels
as you breathe the sage scented air
of the late summer in Italy,
where even the flowers sing.

VIRGINS IN THE UFFIZI

In the morning she said she was tired
of seeing naked men,
but Italy didn't listen.
We were in *Firenze*, walking to
the *Piazza della Signori*
on the way to the *Uffizi*
which she called the penis museum.
She had just turned eighteen
with her hair still in braids
and she was not unlike
the Botticelli maiden
speaking flowers.

The aging Italian goddess
who is our guide
leads us through corridors of
Giotto, Botticelli, Leonardo and Tintoretto
with a sense of humor,
her red nail polish laughing
through her sandals.
She says that Michelangelo's paintings
are really sculptures in one dimension
and asks us to pay attention to the way
Titian and Caravaggio use paint to capture light.

With a smile that seems to fold inward,
she discusses how Renaissance art
went back to the earlier gods, resurrected
the light in the human body.
It's inspiring, overwhelming,
but after two days of naked marble men,

my eighteen-year-old friend
finds herself looking at men on the street
the wrong way.

In the afternoon we walk to
Boboli Gardens at *Palazzo Pitti*,
pay homage to Venus of the Birds.
The pigeons can make a fool of anything
including sculpted marble.
They sit on the head of Adonis,
peck at Hercules' shoulders,
nest on Neptune's uncovered private parts.
They tease Diana and bite her fingers.

My braided friend throws bread
to glowing silver carp in the dirty pond.
A pregnant cat rubs against her knees
while Venus gazes forever at Adonis
in this Florentine Eden.
On the other side of the railing,
a moat, pomegranates, fig trees,
and raked gravel walkways
that humans are not allowed to enter.

In the pond below, pigeons are speaking
to the gods of Eden.
They fly from frog to peacock
at the feet of a water nymph.
On the hills of *Firenze,*
rows of olive trees
and relics of too many wars.
The clouds are puffed tortellini
sliced carelessly
over an Eden of orange and lemon trees.

We walk back on streets from earlier centuries,
but crossing the bridge at *Ponte Vecchio*
a man with eyes made for a movie
catches hers. He pulls her into the sculpture
of his high Roman cheekbones, tries to
seduce her with the charm of his
curly Italian hair
and a few words of broken English.
She wonders how it might be
to run off with him somewhere. And words
are not the only language.

In the evening, she decides not to go
to see the statue of David.
Enough is enough, and Michelangelo
can wait until she is older.
But *Firenze* is full of statues.
At the end of any shaded walkway
always lovers embracing,
but that will come later.

Venetian Blinds

1.   It Echoes

The taxi driver takes me back
to a place where
I don't live anymore.

He is Vietnamese.
I am shimmering, an Egyptian
beaded scarf echoing red
around my face.

I serve him tea on a pashmina shawl
where light streams in
through the slats
of a high Moroccan window.

I cover him with kisses
and linden flowers.

2.   Among Turtles

You used to believe in the things
you argue against now.

You wrestle with me
as if you are arguing
with your own soul –
turtles in your living room
swimming against the glass.

You aren't sure if you want
to make love to me.

And the voices in your head
like turtles
pull you in opposite directions –
one is spiritual
one wants other things.

Last Tuesday you were in the shower
while a funnel cloud
split the center of your street,
ripping trees.

Today the telephone men
are putting up the lines,
but it will take time
before your heart
will speak to you again.

3.　At the Circus

You find me at the circus
dreaming in calliope circles
on the merry-go-round.

Before the music stops
you lift me off the amethyst
horse with silver wings.

In a red velvet room
with chandeliers
you hold me close
as we dance the tango.

38

You ask me to marry you
but I would have had to consent
before I knew you this well.

4.　　My Hair is Full of Tornadoes

I've just come out of a tornado
shelter. The sky is still
dark with warnings.

My hair is full of tornadoes.
He's leaning on my shoulder.

He's older than he wants to be
but there's a tenderness between us.
You can see it in the shoulders
and the way we are leaning together
after the storm.

Our mothers are too fragile —
emotions flapping like laundry
inside a circular wind.

The sky is still dark with thunder
but there's a tenderness
inside.

ENTERING THE WORD TEMPLE

1.   Bird Face

A lacework of yellow oak leaves
in front of the porch of a woman
who paints visions on the walls.

Her colors are from a different place.

The man in her vision has wings
flying over the city of music
with the face of an Egyptian
mythological bird.

The city has a sand bridge
over a blue river.

If she paints him,
he will find her.

2.   Amethyst Birds

He broke four of her windows
before he painted her house.

Around her windows
he painted amethyst birds
flying to South America.

He hid photographs under her pillow
while the house became
lantern green and violet.

Autumn was unseasonably warm.
The wind came from South America,
made his body strong with desire
and conflicted longing.

Hundreds of ladybugs flew
in through the cracked windows.
She counted the spots on their wings.

Everything in her house
is covered by a thin layer of dust –
even the glass hummingbird
in her dreams.

3. Bear Song

As the season changes
the edges of the leaves
are on fire.

The Earth is getting colder,
entering the empty space.

In a loft apartment
a cello
a single note
of a Bach partita
the cadence of an Italian
song.

Each day
I find the single note
that vibrates.

4. Snow Dream

The snow comes out of season
swirling around a wrought-iron street lamp
twenty years ago.

I wake up from a dream
of pelicans and flamingos.
My skin is full of flamingos.

The women are covered with scars,
each one a city,
a citadel, an island.

My skin is rose pink.

I am running barefoot
on a beach of round stones.

I am in the air –
a butterfly, a meadowlark
an open window.

5. Early Playford

Before he replaced the glass,
he sanded the edges of my windows.
The sand came from South America.

On a silver music stand
the *Bach Suites for Cello Solo,*
Early Playford
speaking to my hands.

I find sand in unexpected places.
Inside a vase of swirled blue glass.
Falling out of sand dollars.
Inside hiking socks with a memory
of the Pacific Ocean.

We walk over a wood bridge
after midnight. In the sky
Orion, the Pleiades, Cassiopeia.

Orion shoots his arrow
with sand falling out of his belt.

6.   Chrysanthemums

The cold is delayed.
In November, pink chrysanthemums
still blooming.

There are extra days for painting.

My house is layered with new colors —
lavender, purple and lantern green,
what I see inside
the color of music.

Beyond the open window
the edges of the leaves,
a river of earth and sky
spinning like Sufi women
surrounded by morning glories
and galaxies.

7.   Cello Lesson

In the middle of the forest
I am wearing a black velvet gown.

Muddy print of leaves
on a hidden path,
an amethyst, an echo, a memory.

Inside a grove of pine trees
he plays the cello,
gives his music to the trees.
The song he plays
is for me.

The kiss surprises me.

Music from the pyramids.
Secrets burned
inside the Alexandrian Fire.

Red squirrel
walking on thin branches
through an open window.

ASCENDING

For Grandma Helen

I like to think of her up there
with my grandfather,
standing in a field sweet with blossoming
white corn, cucumbers and tomatoes on the vine
above the clouds.

I see her standing in grey suede pumps
and a tailored suit,
the way she looked when I was a girl,
holding my grandfather's hand.
By her heels her two dogs,
Gretchen and Frieda,
a lazy group of dappled cows grazing
in the green and shimmering
distance.

We spread out a linen table cloth
she wove on the loom in her attic
for a picnic. We are joined
by Ria's grandmother, her basket overflowing
with herbs and flowers from the hills
of South Africa, a bottle of wine,
loaves of bread, goat cheese.
They are humming African melodies with
a spiral of a cloud
wisping above the mountain.

My grandmother is weaving
a linen of sky and clouds,
the blue thread like a jet stream
expanding into the shimmering
dawn. She is gazing up at a dragonfly,
the arc of dew beaded on
a morning glory leaf

in the early morning sunlight.
Two Shepherd puppies chase each other
between the meadowlarks below.
For a moment, she has forgotten everything
except how to sing.

In the summer kitchen, my grandmother
is canning green tomatoes
with the recipe she learned
when she was nine years old
from great-grandmother Lena.
She is slicing onions, stirring a marinade of
dill seeds, brown sugar, and sweet
cider vinegar.

My brothers and I are playing marbles
with beet purple eggs
we refuse to eat.
I am fourteen years old,
Ron is seven, David is five.
We are sunning ourselves on the dock
of the pond that seemed so big to us.
We are swimming in black inner tubes
to cool ourselves from the summer sun,
dragonflies skimming the water
inside a cacophony of bullfrogs.

Grandma Helen, we toast to you
with goblets of Merlot –
my brothers, my father, my mother,
everyone who held you dear –
as you walk through a field of sweet williams,
four o'clocks and tiger lilies.
This spring I am planting pink dianthus
and sunflowers in my garden,
flowers you loved so much
weaving through the hands of your granddaughter
who will always bless you.

Requiem for a Pond

The prairie grasses are starting to grow back
in the vacant field under the arching
Japanese bridge
where the koi pond used to be.

The hot summer winds move across
patches of red clover,
goldenrod and hepatica
where beaver and muskrat
built bridges across
the tributaries of a stream.

Goodbye to evening walks
clapping my hands on the bridge,
tossing pieces of fresh-baked bread
to the carp and catfish.

Goodbye to elderberry blossoms
in humid summer heat,
cicadas in loud cacophony
rising and swelling
through moonlight streaming ribbons
across the humid air.

Farewell to long-necked swans
who led their babies
across these shallow waters,
to the lone Canada goose
breathing her last gasp of air.

Farewell to weddings in the pagoda
by the water.

Farewell to the black water snake,
the bending arms of the weeping
willow, the lantern yellow
underbellies of box turtles.

Goodbye to the *unh unh unh*
of bullfrogs.

Goodbye to the green wings
of hummingbirds above sunflowers,
lilies, and black-eyed Susans,
to the blue whirring
of dragonflies skimming the water.

Farewell to new lovers
walking over the arching bridge
for the first time together. Farewell
to solitary dreamers longing for hands.
Farewell to my reflection
in the water.

The night they drained the pond
students carried the fish
in bowls and buckets
to the closest river.

Now the wind is a paintbrush
over the memory of water.

Goodbye to constellations
reflected to an earth
that is sleeping.

Children play hide and seek
in the woods where
they're cutting down old growth trees
to build new houses.
Farewell to the memory
of tree frogs.

Candle boats scatter roses
below an evening
swimming with fireflies.
Goodbye to the full moon
reflected on these waters.

Goodbye to the souls
of the trees.

Fourth of July in Fairfield, Iowa

Watching the fireworks with Nancy Berg,
I like the ones that fizzle
and fall into the reservoir.
The fireflies are confused, unfocused,
knocking their heads on the Queen Anne's lace.
The Pleiades have turned red
and now are slowly sinking beyond the horizon
like seven flamboyant women in the boys' shower.
Behind us the blonde haired farm girls are going wild.
Light another one! Light another one! Light another one!
Just like the Statue of Liberty holding a pinwheel.
Just like Niagara Falls spilling over Nancy's hair,
slinky fiddle music, turning to its own direction.
This one is dedicated to the computer nerds in Fairfield.
This one is the astronomy map in Pod 123,
mysterious candles on an exploding birthday cake,
a *Classics Illustrated* comic imploded into the future,
finally recognized, painted years ago
in defiance of *Mad Magazine* by Mrs. Berg.
Nancy's boyfriend buys us lemonade.
Afterwards, they will play on the swings,
go home, and not make love.
The frat boys from the edges of hell
toilet paper the elm tree by the courthouse.
I leave my windows open
and wait for flamingos
at four o'clock in the morning.

THEY THOUGHT IT WAS A DRAGON KITE

For Martha Ho

Waiting for the L
three blocks from the Pacific,
green wave crashing
down the slope to Taraval Beach,
they thought it was a dragon kite
but really it was a river
of old Chinese women.

Noisy flock of seagulls
arcs north toward the Headlands
above a spider web mesh
of electric wire.
Dragon kite flirts with pelican
above sand dollar
littered beach.

Flock of Cantonese women
in baseball caps
gathers at the bus stop,
chirps like paper cranes in a language
that floated here on wooden boats.
They fly on silver tracks
to Chinatown vegetable markets.

When I am ninety-eight years old,
I want to ride to Paradise
in a river of multi-ethnic women
singing in a kite of languages
on dragons with silver wings
lifting like Sun and Moon
to the apogee, then the edge
of a blue horizon.

Want to fly above silver tracks.
Don't want to ride there
on a streetcar!

51

Chagall in the City of Angels

WHAT MY BETTA FISH IS DREAMING

Fishface was lonely when I went to work today. He was thinking about the orange flamboyance of his fins and whether that really makes him the center of attention. Orange and silver fanfare, circling and circling. And can a betta fish be the eye of a spherical galaxy in a bowl with no one looking, dancing for his pleasure alone?

Fishface contemplates issues of audience. Is the stage a platform for connection with an audience or a bowl to swim in circles of the self? And does music come from colored stones, glassy and transparent? Fishface dreams he is a salmon or a rainbow trout, cascading down a waterfall. He dreams he is an echo in an abandoned redwood forest.

Fishface is writing a novel as stones are falling. Or maybe it's snow. He dreams he is in Nepal, sixteen seconds before an avalanche. The world is getting colder, and the branches of rhododendron trees are sheathed in ice. The sun fills the icefall with light until the edges fall from their own weight. Fishface has past life memories of being a trilobite. The Kali Gandaki River Gorge is an ice littered war zone.

Fishface thinks I am a flying fish in a larger tank. He watches me eat breakfast. He'd like to swim to me if he could float through glass. He reads *The New Yorker* and admires a poem by Rustin Larson. He flashes my reflection on his silver fin. He dreams of swimming in Alaska with the Northern Lights spilling across the sky.

Fishface doesn't take personal growth seminars. He doesn't get blamed for the things that go wrong in his life. In his singular bowl lined with blue glass stones, he is unaware that betta fish in pairs fight each other to the death. His fins are beautiful.

Fishface isn't a part of anyone's late night mythology. He doesn't send holiday gifts, and he won't surprise you with a phone call after too many years have obscured the memory of his face. He doesn't ride the Tilt-A-Whirl or distort himself in fun house mirrors.

Fishface will dream of eels tonight taking shapes he hasn't seen. A thousand bettas, newly born, swim out of a coral cave, unaware of snow, branch or stone. In the morning, he will wait patiently for tiny globes of fish food that fall like stars from my fingers. In my quiet joy, I will listen to the tiny crunch of his teeth.

AFTER SHE FELL FROM THE SUMMIT OF THE BODY SCULPTURE

"People forget how beautiful
to live on this earth."
Hunter Bahnson

On the other side of the mirror
a fire is floating.

Before she returns from darkness,
the light is saturated in red
like a rose petal
or something in her body
she hasn't discovered yet.

She had a concussion that summer.
That's what the doctor said
when he examined her eyes,
her pupils wide,
dark brown like the earth
where she fell.

For the next month
her family muffled the light.
Inside the green curtain
memory was a thin veil.

Her memories were jumbled –
leaves falling through water.
She sang to the dolphins
through double exposures
hidden from the sun.

In her sleep
she called out names of flowers —
redbud, clematis, hydrangea,
white orchid.

The dolphins took her to rocks
shaped like camels and pterodactyls.
She could swim there
if the waves weren't too high
if the sand wasn't dreaming
if the rocks weren't
wet with seals.

All night she swam with the dolphins.
She saw visions inside of caves —
stone choreographies,
stalagmites, harem dancers.

They wandered
in and out of green waves,
jade islands, a calligraphic map.

She swam through a season of roses
with the dolphins
and came back floating —
a girl in a red silk skirt,
a dancer with silver fish
swimming through her hands,
a shape that only water
could create.

At the edge
the ocean was silver,

constellations swirling, the clouds
massive, swimming
like dolphins.

Her world is curved now.
No edges.
Blue frog prints on the rocks.
The sun always rising
inside the lavender petals
of an orchid.

BELLY DANCE

The floor where I sleep
is covered with leaves and music.
My bed is surrounded with candles,
the dream light heightened
and shimmering.

I invite you into a white room.
I wear a white dress.
I light a candle.
I cover myself with coconut oil
and rose petals.

I am the white lace cloud of beauty,
a forbidden love of red roses,
the echo of silver bells,
Egyptian camel blankets,
the subtle curve of forgotten coastlines.

Your back is a eucalyptus tree.
A starling flies out of the branches.
I rub out the knots
with my elbows
as leaves are falling.

After you leave
in the late summer fog,
I play a painted flute.
In my music, the change of season
is a catalyst for memory.

Already you are part way
up the mountain. In the fire

of a scented candle,
you will kiss the petals of my face,
and reach for the Egyptian
coastline of my hip.

TSUNAMI

For Robin Lim

A scar the shape of a crescent moon
floats above my left ankle.
Through the winter I dance
in silver ankle bracelets from India
a dead man gave me.

His kiss made me restless.
A star streaked across the sky
leaving a wake of cold,
a burning the physical mind
cannot annihilate
as the fear changes to worship.

Back in Iowa, a change of seasons.
Cottonwood floats in the air
falling like snow,
dreams on the wing of a gypsy moth,
a trail of thistles,
the memory of shimmering
heat waves on the silos
next to the Kalona Cheese factory.

The midwife is eating salad.
I put an olive on her plate
as her house fills with friends
and their children.
Merlot spills in the kitchen
as the men sing
I'm Lookin' for a Love
in giddy red wine harmony.

The muse plays a hammered
dulcimer as though she
is cutting string beans.
She says, "I've trained my friends
to be satisfied
with little bits of me."

Now she is gone to Bali
but I hear her voice
in the sun, moon, wind and rain.

THE GODDESS OF MIDNIGHT

"You've been walking into the mystery.
I've been walking into the bones."

Nancy Hensil

1.

I saw the comet last night,
streaming through space in a cascade
of wild blue hair –
the Goddess of Midnight.
Dancing in a vapor trail,
streaking a blue path in the dark night.

I had trouble falling asleep,
and a shower didn't help.
There were particles of blue flying Goddess
all around my skin.
Something newly released from my bones
hovered above my bed.
Maybe it was the hologram of his chest
and his shoulders too far away.

2.

In Tel Aviv we are eating
pita bread and *hummos*.
The holograms of our lives are round
like pita bread.
The center is the same,
but the life paths are different.

We gather sticks in *I Ching* hexagrams.
Waiting.   Courting.

Difficult at the beginning.
The Receptive.   The Return.

I gather stones from the sand
on the North Shore of Lake Michigan.
The stones are round,
but the veins are different.

The stones say
waiting is not mere empty hoping.
She should let herself be led.
The light comes back
at the time of the Winter Solstice.

3.

I am the Goddess of Midnight.
I flew through fire for you
in a wash of blue comet feathers.
I loved you while the moon
rose and fell. While the tides
fell back into the sea. But you
were a cedar tree and you
stayed a stranger.

So I become a woman again.
I fly to Oregon, hike with dragonflies,
cool myself under cedar trees in
the Columbia River Gorge.
I swim in the currents of
Horsetail Falls. Triple Falls.

In the late afternoon
I walk through fields of maiden hair ferns,

wild orchids and hydrangeas,
but my heart is falling over water.

4.

The silver plane circles back
flies over your house
and leaves the North Shore.

I expected someone long ago
but there's been a mix-up
or a delay. Maybe it's Iowa.

All winter I bring the *I Ching*
into bed with me,
but there aren't any messages.

My dreams have transparent edges.
The stones say I am open and present
but not owned. No blame.

On the way to the airport,
I see omens in animals —
white horse pushing out of a barbed wire fence.
Two brown cows in a meadow.
Redwing blackbird flying free.

5.

Climbing hills in San Francisco
feels like waking up
from a strange dream.
But this dream has too many tattoos,
too much piercing,

even though the henna shop in the Mission
is Eastern and temporary.

The hills speak to me
in the language of calla lilies.
Climbing the winding paths above the fog,
my legs are singing.
More definition in my muscles
from hiking the trails above Muir Woods.
More definition in my muscles
from nights of dancing.

In the kitchen
I cut red cabbage.
The knife reveals secret passageways,
hidden rooms full of dreams,
a man and a women
trying to remember the shapes
and colors of flowers they have forgotten.
They have become aware of each other
but only in dreams.
They are connected by a thin thread of light
that weaves through corridors
of red cabbage.

In her sleep she crosses the Equator,
circles back with toucans,
has lunch by the Dead Sea.
The mountains are full of scrolls
with secret messages. She is certain
the mountain knows his name.

At Ein Gedi she sees shapes in the waterfall,
but she wakes up in the desert
before she sees his face.

At four o'clock in the morning
the stones speak the language of mountains.
I am older now
in a way I don't understand.
Emotions undiscovered. Philosophy unexplored.
And the silver thread lost
connecting these two worlds.
The stones say the future
will reveal itself in pieces,
and I have to wait.

The man and the woman
are trying to find each other.
He speaks in philosophy. She speaks in images.
The stones say they need to create a new language.
She is the moon. He is a cedar tree.
Their words are full of stones and light
and red cabbage.

6.

He said that music is something about
coming into a body
and taking on physical form.
Finding a shape for the spirit.
On the cello vibrato comes from the heart.
It gives shape to emotion and joy.
The arm is only the heart's echo.

I dream in a wooden house on a mountain
with a little horse.
The house is surrounded by stones
with mica prisms refracting the sunlight.
The horse gives birth to another
horse in a dream.

I am the midwife and somehow also
the horse at the same time.

My friends come back from the hills
of calla lilies.
It is getting dark, so I put
the little horse to sleep in a basket.
Her skin is rose pink,
and I sing to her all night.

The clouds are white mackerels
floating across the sky.
They float through tunnels of wind
where I hear you breathing.
The clouds take the shape of the man
I haven't seen yet.
I hear him singing in midnight language.
I swim in the echo of his collarbone.

I sing to you from the hollow
of my shoulder blade,
from the resonance of the tea rose,
from the wood inside the f-curves
of my cello, softly scented
like your skin after loving.

7.

Loving is a dance of desire and fear.
Balance and swing.
Apart.   Together.
With the tip of your paintbrush,
you reach across the distances
through wind tunnels,
and the dreams you have been hiding
shape my face.

After the new moon
we are kayaking on the Tuolumne River.
The birds are omens —
cormorant,
        snowy egret,
                blue heron.
Ospreys nesting in the trees
by the side of the river.

Under the blue echo of a comet,
our room is a lacework of branches.
Through the forest, light is floating
from the moon.

We dance under redwood trees,
and the visions we have been holding
for so many years
ascend like comets
into the thin layer of sky
where electron storms become
aurora borealis.

CHAGALL IN THE CITY OF ANGELS

Paint your apartment
orange, yellow and blue.
Hang the things you used to love
from the crossbeams
on your ceiling.

Cut off amber curls
from your hair.
Buy a round pair of glasses.

Paint an icon of lovers
on the wall.
Make love on the futon.

In the city light
which hides the full moon,
become what you paint.

You are a blue clown.
She has melon moon breasts
and red hair.
A dog or a cow plays the violin.

Visit the neighbor
who bakes you sweet
pear pies.

In the morning
brew tiny black leaves
of tea she gave you
from Sri Lanka.

Put on a Tibetan
t-shirt.

Take a bath full of herbs
in the lions paw tub.

MARKET STREET ANGEL

"Approach pain and suffering
with curiosity and tenderness"
Buddhist Saying

Mostly rich people go to the Symphony.
At the pre-concert talk, the conductor
calls the canon we will hear
a musical handshake across six centuries.
He says if you listen closely,
the music will reveal its secrets.
The violins swell like ocean waves,
green and crashing through the moon.

The conductor is an acrobat, an astronaut,
a genius, but in the second tier
the sound is too small.
My friend who plays trumpet at other concerts
leans over the balcony
to get closer, and I wonder
what would happen here in an earthquake.

After the symphony,
a beggar with chocolate eyes
reminds me of a saint, except
he wants something from you.
No. No. Not pears or oranges. Please money.
And Karla, the woman
who sings at the BART station,
has gotten too thin.
The sores on her face have crescendoed,
and she looks suddenly
ten years older.

On the streetcar, old Chinese women
move closer to the door
to escape from the drunk man
who reeks of urine.
They all live in my neighborhood
and will be riding
to the end of the line,
where Mama Ocean's ebb and flow
drifts in through the open
skylight.

At the Haight Street Circus,
nineteen year olds with shaved heads,
henna tattoos, and pierced navels
wait for nothing at the corner.
By the Red Victorian Theatre,
a tall woman in 7-inch
leopard spike heels
wears a leather miniskirt that reveals
too many secrets.

Karla,
with sores on her face,
has migrated from the BART station.
She gets on the 71
to spend a night at the beach.
Like anyone who lives on the street,
all of her secrets are gone.

She rolls out her sleeping bag
on the sand
where a Goddess Moon
shines her light on everyone.

Her body is holding on
to a thin row of stars
that is leaving for the Pleiades.
Her voice is already on
a distant journey, but she sings
until three o'clock in the morning.

LESSONS IN ASTRONOMY

1.

The loft where I am sleeping
dissolves
and you have gone to Jupiter.

The Solstice leaves
a waning moon,
the push pull of emotional
gravity.

The memory is an asteroid
and Saturn has eighteen moons.

2.

He wrote a waltz for me
called *Earth Embrace*.
The music came
whenever he closed his eyes
and thought of me.

We danced
climbing up the mountain,
leaf shadows on the path,
breathing eucalyptus.
We stopped at the edge of the
ridge trail, filling our buckets
with huckleberries.

The memory is a thundercloud
filled with light.

3.

South is the best direction for wind.
It blows warm in November.

The midheaven moon
is covered by
shattered charcoal cloud,
later full behind oak leaves,
a geisha with her hand
over her mouth.

4.

The man who said
he would spend his life with me
can't keep his promise.

My heart is a drum
beating from Jerusalem,
and nobody speaks this language.

On the airplane
I carry a gift of lavender irises.
There isn't a seat for my cello,
so I hold it between my knees.

5.

Under the full moon
a shaman lifts my feet
out of lavender water,
out of the Nile River mud.

He covers me
with Eucalyptus oil.

On the horizon, a row of camels
moving against the moon,
the cool night air
condensing against the pyramids.

At midnight
he puts a pear slice
in my mouth,
covers my face
with a fine white powder.

HIKING BY THE HUDSON RIVER

Grief layers my body
with shields of lavender light.
I walk into the forest
to the hidden place
where the deer are nesting.

I follow the deer
to learn how leg is connected
to shoulder.
I lean toward the East
and the deer licks my spine.

I am looking for a new language,
a new way of being in the world.
I hike further to the clearing
inside a cathedral of spruce trees
where two hawks circle
in an updraft of coastal wind.

Happiness floats where the sky
meets the hawks flying.
I follow the curve of the wing
in slow circles.

I walk on stones
crossing a tiny creek with the current
stopped by a beaver dam.
Before the pool releases,
the water fills with images
from another country.

On the other side of the world,
a man with wide cheekbones.
Two deer leap over
his round face. At his ankles
flowers I cannot name,
layered with lavender.

Rain drips from the branches
as he speaks in a different language
stories of water buffalo.
His voice finds a quiet place
inside the wound.

WHEN THEIR LOVE LEAKS THROUGH THE CEILING

1.

Their dream comes through the wall
in the morning as his girlfriend
walks out of his house
for the last time.

My wall is covered with beetles
that flew from the East.
He says he will call the exterminator
while I ride on a streetcar
from the ocean to the bay.

We sit outside watching sunflowers
in the four o'clock wind.

He says, "I'm losing the love of my life."
I say, "I wish it could be different."

Our neighbor is playing *Shnei Shoshanim,*
a song I used to dance to.
He sits close to me,
wraps his hands around my knees.

Before I leave, he says,
"Listen to your messages."

2.

I play cello
and let the notes rise
through the ceiling
while they make love.

The vibrato weaves through
a pattern of stars on my legs,
explodes into asteroids
slides into dolphins
swimming warm against the current.

She says she's moving back to Wisconsin
or maybe she'll fly to Thailand.

He told me, "She wouldn't talk about it."
She said, "It's not my way."

Last night I was laughing with friends
in the living room. I wanted to
bring them *sake* on a tray of irises,
leave it warm
outside their bedroom door.

At midnight I open the skylight
and listen to waves crash
under a waning moon.

But night is a mystery,
a dream of a woman, a nautilus shell,
and the thousand ways
the body desires to be loved.

3.

When their love leaks through the ceiling,
I dream I am on the North Shore
of Chicago. It's winter, and I
am watching the smaller waves of
Lake Michigan crash
on the ice around the stones.

My ceiling is inches away
from where they make love.

I am dancing with a shaman
but he isn't able to read
the cracks on the inner walls
of the stones.

My ceiling dissolves
into sand dunes rising from
early morning fog.

I am riding a streetcar
to the Pacific Ocean.

Saint-Saens' violin music
drifts across the sand.
Wood on the beach is burning
before the gray whales migrate
to Antarctica.

POURING SAND

Before I went back to Iowa,
you gave me two jars of sand
so I would remember the ocean.
We drove together, for you
a first vision of snow
over the mountains, an exodus
during the year of bleeding.

And what is love? A heartbeat in the ear?
A meditation of light?
A bear dance on the ecliptic
at the end of a century?
Voice of the angels. Timpani of stars.
Symphony of bones.

I took herbs for the bleeding —
tansy, motherwort,
comfrey, yellowdock, myrrh,
graperoot, cayenne.
My arms stretched too far in dancing,
fingers out of phase, legs angled
from the hip. Memory of poppies,
the tone of singing bowls,
of bells.

You had to lead the dance,
pumping iron in my living room.
Belly to the floor.
A blue cup, an excuse
during the exile to Babylonia.

You say I stayed away too long.
I say you didn't wait.
A river we crossed.
Yes, I know, you're the kind of man
who needs to have someone.

In the season of elderberries,
meteor showers, memories fall like snow.
Maple seeds shower down like sperm
looking for a place to plant themselves.
In a warm wind, oriental poppies
during the week of the bloom.

I paint my toes red, feet gently rocking
inside the fence of a farm house
on the old porch swing.

I continue along the ecliptic,
performing small acts of homeopathic
magic, a harem dancer
below an eclipse of the moon
inside sapphire blue light.

What I don't understand
is overwhelming
as I run out in the rain,
pulling pottery out of the hutch,
the rooster pitcher, the hand crafted
raku bowl of green tea,
glaze embedded in lavender.
I leave these on your porch
between the wood and the broken
screen door.

In the morning I pour the sand
into my garden – around three shells
from the Pacific Ocean.
My own little beach.
You're on the way to Hawaii
with the new love you've found.
I need to be free.

WOMAN WITH A GREEN DONKEY

BEES

He doesn't have a name anymore, only his childhood memories of catching bees inside jars and forgetting to poke holes in the lid. The bees would circle inside the glass, around and around until they died. Sometimes at night he'd catch a jar full of fireflies and open the lid in his bedroom — his private collection of constellations and shooting stars. Later he'd roll down hills, around and around until he was too dizzy to walk, to apologize to the bees.

We went to the reservoir that January afternoon and held each other in a frozen white world. Frost on the brown weeds, frost on the prairie grass. Something pierced by bees opened in me as I listened to his apologies. We sat in class together for three weeks until he suddenly stopped coming. There was a snowstorm that night, and his friends asked me to find him and see if he was warm enough.

The lights were out when I came to his room. I knocked on the door before I heard the sighing of a woman, a voice like snow. He came to the door before I could run away to tell me they were going back to California. It was very sudden, he said, but real. I walked back into the snow through muffled shapes under streetlights.

For the rest of the winter, I knit a scarf at night, weaving sunflower yellow, sky blue and lavender, but with bands of other colors left over from the collages of my friends, who were mainly dancers, sculptors, and musicians. The winter was unusually cold — the snow piled deeper through February and March.

When I move back to San Francisco, I join a dance troupe. A tall man with blue eyes falls in love with me, but I'm not who he wants me to be. He teases me about being too cautious crossing streets, but he doesn't have a passport. I fly to Nepal with a tent and hike in the mountains. He turns into a bee when I am dreaming and stings me.

I have a friend who believes she won't be happy with a man she is fully attracted to. I watch her thoughts create her husband. She doesn't like the way he smells, but he adores her, thinks she's magic. She rolls down hills full of bees. My grandmother says, "Never sleep with a man who gives you nightmares. And if you are afraid, walk in the direction of the bees."

Two Rivers

1.

Old train bridge in Tennessee
mountain music
and a man with hazel eyes
rivers valleys and art
in his hands.

He sees me in a yellow dress
swirling. It's a crossover point.

All weekend, dancing in stars and rings
bass old timey rhythm
vibrating the barn dance floor
sending signals to the silo
below an ice-hazed moon.

And the waltz
inside a crowded room
with nothing in focus
except his eyes.

No war in Iraq
sign at the corner,
paper whites
on the back porch.

We're worried that the world
is going to explode.

Ceylon breakfast tea,
an orange star necklace

around my neck,
glitter circles, glitter smile
hands that tell a story.

He's a wild pony —
kissing me in the time zone
where days begin
and days are torn apart.

2.

Exposed to laryngitis by kissing,
I dance through the weekend.

Above us, the Pleiades,
Scorpion, Milky Way, Snow Moon
distant stars releasing.

The shaman is a donkey
glueing a mirror
to pieces of a dream.

Road full of ice on the way home.
We drive into the snow.
Stop sign
where I don't want to leave.

Shaman says love is an elephant,
dead weight on the road.
She says thank the elephant
by kicking him sometime.

She says love is impractical,
wants to unhook the pony

let him float off without a cloud
singing, light of heart
and load.

I tell her love
is slow moving cinema
etched with a charcoal pencil,
sweet smooth dancing
with the ending hidden by mist.

The shaman says,
"Don't put a horse trailer
behind your Toyota."

3.

Back in Iowa,
glitter of paperwhites in my dreams
as the nation is preparing
for a war we don't want.

He sees me in a yellow dress
swirling inside a snow storm
cutting origami paper
into snowflakes.

I dance with him under
Northern skies
splashed with the aurora.

Across six hundred miles
we breathe in lindy circles
orbits of jagged steps
in a swing dance.

Fantail of my betta fish
swirling over blue stones
in the kitchen.
Cardinal on the oak
tells me to leap over the hills
and kick the donkey.

Waiting for you.
Doing the elephant walk.
Inhaling the steam
of eucalyptus.

I'd like to keep my voice
this time. If my fingers
knew how to texture
light and shadow,
I would draw your face.

RIVERS OF LIGHT

"A white rain.
Then your face becoming another's..."
                              Carolyn Forche

Rivers of light flow through your hands.
This might be about memory
or the imprint of molecules
you gave me
in a rust-colored pickup truck.

My emotions fill with lavender
the way music triggers memory —
a String Dancer waltz in Kentucky
your artist arms circling around
my heart, giving gyroscopic signals
I can't interpret right now.

I want to tell you about the way
blackberry vines are pushing up
from my garden, how the sky is warmer now.
I dream through the next weekend
clearing leaves from my garden
as early tulips and columbine
leaves unfold.

I want you to see the way
my hair gets curly and wild
in the humid April heat.
I'd like to ask you questions.

Around my pillow at night
the orbit of a humid empty space.

And in the emptiness, the singing
of a cello, a tremolo voice saying
Love it. Hold the memory.
Fill it with light and singing.
Fill it with your face.

Your eyes change color
to match the emerging leaves,
a river of sky,
the bark of an olive tree.
They cannot see lavender.

I'd like to tell you about red paint
inside a canoe of memory
in a dream I had. And I wonder
how you feel with a charcoal
pencil in your hand.

The lines that shape muscles
get lost inside themselves –
a kinesthetic history of cross-beams
a bridge over the Ohio River,
on the dance floor
your hand slipping up
the bare place on my spine.

What color are your eyes?
We need to take a journey.
My dreams fill with lavender –
an echo, a flood, a space shuttle.
What else can't you see?

The future is hidden
inside the trajectory of asteroids,
across the Plum Creek River,
flowing by a red rock arch
under oak leaves.

BELLS OF BRUNATE

Wet leaves drift to the pavement
in early morning light.
A cloud hovers over Lake Como,
disintegrates into the echo of bells,
then lifts to reveal the morning.

You eat goat cheese and bread
under the shade of a red tile roof
between rows of ginkgo trees,
drunk with more than wine
on a woven blanket.

The sun shimmers the lake
as you hike higher up the mountain
in Italy, where art is wine
that can make you drunk with color
and angels for weeks.

The old gate keeper
who guards the stone tower
opens the green door
and invites you to the moon.

The bells drift up from the *Duomo*.
The donkey's mouth is a crescent
moon. And the woman
with olive tree arms
growing around his neck
curls her long blue hair
into a Botticelli waterfall.

WOMAN WITH A GREEN DONKEY

After Chagall

The woman with blue hair
  says she's turned him
   into a donkey.

He is her muse,
  and she's riding him
   to the Moon.

They wrap themselves
  around statues
   as though they were floating islands
    or trails on mountains.

The muse is a donkey.

When they marry,
  Chagall is the donkey
   inside the moon
    who serenades them.

Chagall is the painter
  playing a blue violin
   under their feet.

BATIK GODDESSES

The message is printed in orange crayon:
stones across a river
a hair brush for her granddaughter
a Balinese melody ascending
from the f-holes of a cello.

Chu-Chu gives me a hand
full of yarrow blossoms
pale pink, white and green
growing through ferns
on the sarong she wears.

In her medicine bag
a black butterfly wing
with a river of fire
cut through,
a purple crayon.

Her words
resonate like Tibetan bells
around my shoulders.
They float through my legs
They come from somewhere else.

At night, Chu-Chu puts lavender
under my pillow. I dream
of turquoise hummingbird wings
against a lavender sky.
They fly through my sarong.

Two-thirds of a moon
over a koi pond
ascending

as she wraps a batik
orchid around my hips.

The monkey god is playing violin,
juggling tomatoes,
placing them like jewels
around my feet.

TURTLE WOMAN

For Ruth Stone

As the gods were stealing her vision,
she fell into her words, face first
into the book she wrote.
Singing as she tumbled toward
the darkness, as
a grasshopper jumped over
her long red hair.

Each morning
waking up through a hail storm.
Each morning, finding new light
through the green vision
of a turtle, her voice
a cicada, a frog, a bridge
of stone.

If she loses the green and blue
of the world,
she will see deeper —
salt waves crashing against the lighthouse,
henna painted on the shell
of a stone turtle,
a blue omen, a green gift,
a language stolen from the gods,
dreams thin as a bone
in an old woman's wrist.

INVITATION TO THE LABYRINTH

You give me invisible gifts.

Constantly you instruct me
by who you are
what we don't say
what we don't touch.

We speak to each other
only in gestures of carved
Greek sculpture –
the curve of a shoulder
the innuendo of an elbow
perfectly formed
muscles in the thighs
opening to
the holy place.

You teach me this every day.

In your presence
life has become an art form
a blessing
the open sky of your eyes
bleeding to turquoise
Tibetan stones
opening like a sea of trilobite fossils
to new levels of truth
and understanding.

But even as I speak these words,
a part of you is somewhere else –

Walking the streets of San Francisco
all night, eyes wide open
heart a fragment of blue glass,

the beggars,
like trees on Market Street,
speaking to you –
the black man in a plaid jacket
with a novel in his face,
the saxophone player in a red baseball cap
wailing to a sliver moon.

In the tension between earth and sky
you give yourself to these things
painting the eucalyptus midnight
with your bare chest –
every vision a blessing
a gift.

SLICES OF PAPAYA

"If someone could love me as I am,
I would take off my face."
Sheryl St. Germain

It all dissolves in the morning.

The Milky Way like a banana
Sagittarius rising in the East.
Vega, Antares, Cassiopeia
now your left and right shoulder.
Andromeda, the Crab Nebula
your left and right leg.

Dark bread on a wooden table
in the middle of a forest.
In the distance a path through mint leaves
winding up to the Dolomites.

I write the things I didn't do with you
in calligraphy on my skin.
Slices of tomato
and arugula from the garden.
A dream of oak leaves
I didn't tell.

The fire burns slowly –
papaya scented oil
smoothed on the legs and breast,
the voice of a solitary cricket
singing from a distant cloud.

In a stone house by a river,
tomatoes, basil, and pasta
from the Friday market
simmering on the iron stove,
anchovies swimming in a bucket.

My dreams are walking over a bridge
on a Tuesday evening –
Solstice moon rising over
seven stone houses
in a field of bougainvillea
connected to the wild.

Your eyes swim in a canvas
of Mediterranean light,
waking up to
a dream of sliced papaya,
shadows from the moon
like a lover
sliding through an open window.

THE APOCALYPSO TANTRIC BOYS CHOIR

I walk into The Tea Room
with Robin to see
The Apocalypso Tantric Boys Choir
where my friend David
author of *Zero Gravity Funk Libido*
plays drums.

My ex-boyfriend walks in
with his new girlfriend
in mismatched leopard
and jellyfish sandals.

In an almost empty room,
they sit right in front of me
so that every time I look at the band,
I have to look at them.

I lean over to Robin and whisper,
"He's a misogynist."

My ex and his girlfriend
order two creamy slices of
cheese cake
with a cascade of fresh strawberries
spilling off the top.

They block our view,
even when they
lean away from each other,
which is most of the time.

Abruptly, in the middle of a song,
they get up and leave.
He doesn't notice his keys
are on the floor, next to
their two half finished desserts.

Robin leans over to me and whispers,
"People who don't finish their desserts
don't like oral sex."

After my ex comes back for his keys
and leaves again,
Robin grabs two forks
and both desserts. She eats his
and makes me eat
what his girlfriend left over.

AMBIVALENCE SOUFFLE

After six months
I still can't remember your telephone number,
but this is a metaphor
for the amnesia of love.

Love is a black leather glove
elbow high
but the arm is missing.

I'm burning the screen at the airport
where you turned your head away
when I tried to kiss you.
All the way to San Francisco,
my memories are a movie
of human mating behavior.
I bring out my air picnic bag
of ambivalence souffle.

Love is an asteroid;
the sky is breaking.

On the sky phone
I try to memorize your numbers
with my fingers,
skating my left hand over the keys
like a choreography,
but we are an ice dance.

Love is a pig farm,
and you need to change your socks.

Below out of season
holiday lights
a ring of UFOs hovers above
my heart chakra.
My heart is shining,
so excuse me,
take off your sunglasses.

Love is a hail storm.
The lights have gone out.

On the cell phone
my doctor says,
"Go to the party anyway.
Enjoy the music, flirt,
drink wine."

I am painting the orange flames
of oriental poppies
you didn't have time to see
during the week of the bloom.
Please stop looking
at the pool of blood on my foot.

Love is a freight train,
and I am riding out of here.

Mask Awakening
Egyptian Dream

TENNIS BALLET

For PJS and JM

In my fantasy, they aren't wearing shirts. It's later in the afternoon, cooler, and the light is pushing towards rose pink, like my skin when I am loving you.

The Russian Dancer and the Postman volley a tennis ball. They are playing just for me. I watch them shake hands, spin the racket. The Russian gets the serve. He lifts, dancing, flamboyant, almost fragmented. He is the Norse God Tyr, the God of Fire and Triathlon. On his feet, Nikes, the Messenger God, the Norse God of Commercialism.

The Postman warms up slowly, saving his fire for later. He says he is out of practice, with a deceptive smile. He is a small animal with black fur and eyes that only see after midnight. But when the ball moves towards him, he is intensely focused.

The Russian is more interested in ballet than athletics. He leaps, pirouettes, returns the serve. Suddenly a broken string. Something else is breaking and holding, high up in the air. Now the ball is over the fence. The dancer circles, turns back. He is looking for lost sheep on the hills of Jerusalem.

A yellow jacket hovers into a scrap of light drifting between two trees, gets into attack mode. The Postman delivers a topspin lob, way up in the air and impossible to return. A buzzing circles around me. I have to move, quickly, into the shadows.

The Russian has become a philosopher of drop shots and underspins. He is a sculptor of the unlikely angle. It's more important than winning. He is Plato in the world of ideal forms. Underneath appearances is the most beautiful shot in the world.

The Russian knows that tricky shots are for flirting, and he doesn't save them. He has become a flamingo with slick pink feathers, one eye on the ball, the other watching me. When he cracks the ball, his beak is in his feathers, but the Postman returns everything. They are in the Acropolis – warriors who need each other to pursue excellence. For thousands of years, it's the same conversation. A world where a difficult ball is a compliment.

The tennis ball is a woman with a wide papaya mouth, cutting melon in the Philippines. The Postman is a rock musician, with a grandstand of invisible bystanders going wild. He's on stage, and the redwings are swooning. The butterflies are going wild. But he is not chasing women – he's chasing tennis balls.

In China two monk philosophers are studying the Tao. It's a philosophy of delicate calibrations, slight adjustments. In the slanted light, two dragonflies swirl around Chinese calligraphy. The words ripple. The world as they know it is about to disappear. In the late afternoon, the words disintegrate. The Universe has become round. The monks are two cicadas arcing over the ecliptic, a South wind full of heat and flowers in their face. The tennis ball is a hen house on a Midwestern plain just before a tornado.

Bees fly to the yellow globe, circle the braids of the woman watching from the side. They almost get her. The Russian says, "That's enough violence for one afternoon," but the Postman stops hiding and slices the ball. The dancer can't return it. The ball is a flying cloud, and the sun is almost blinding in the four o'clock heat.

The dancer plays to the audience, shoulders bare, the tennis ball his excuse for a pirouette. The Postman minimizes his Irish cheekbones, plays to himself. At the edge of the field, a bumblebee, a hummingbird, a single falling leaf. At the edge of the mind, a fantasy of a plié.

The tennis ball is six wives, leaping for him at the same time, and he doesn't want any of them. They are dancing for him in a marble pool. A woman with long dark hair covers herself with jasmine blossoms and lets the veils fall, one by one. She is spinning in a rapture. He yawns, takes off his shoes, and silently dances out the back door.

It's different in my fantasy. A volley of Norwegian shoulders, Irish cheekbones, tennis and ballet. The Russian leaping across the stage, the Postman playing a tribal beat on the bass guitar. A hot wind blows in from Africa. In the distance, a singular falling leaf, a butterfly, a plié. The tennis ball flying at the speed of a fighter jet. The butterfly an ascending note of a Bach partita, in and out of the chain link fence. My heart is a faded half moon over an elderberry branch, snowing blossoms.

The Russian calls to the butterfly, slices the ball, but the Postman returns it with an underspin. He's totally cool, on stage, a jazzman with a saxophone, playing a song that is trying to annihilate itself. He is a monk inside a cloister in the fourteenth century, copying scrolls to keep the words from disappearing. It's a philosophy he doesn't understand, and he feels naked, trapped. In his confusion, he smashes the ball. But in order to win, he needs to work on steadiness.

In my fantasy, you do this just for me. We are in a club in Paris, late at night. I am Anais and you are Henry Miller. I am wearing a red feather boa. You are wearing a red baseball cap and red shorts. In a jeweled mirror, I watch your back ripple.

I am a hummingbird in love, hovering over your shoulder. I am the spinning orbit of a philosophy made of bird feathers. All of the men I have ever loved are spinning inside me, in constant pursuit of perfection, some greater excellence unfolding, the artist, the body celebrating, the mind body gap closing, rendering the imaginary art, the perfect shot, the perfect universe, making it real.

The Postman is pedaling up the cliffs of a small island off the coast of Italy. He is in exile on a one-speed bicycle. The tennis ball is a dancer who falls sideways into his arms.

LATE AFTERNOON
IN THE WAKODAHATCHIE WETLANDS

I hold my mother's hand
as we wander through the Wakodahatchie Wetlands.
She moves slowly, a thin blue river,
a turtle on the boardwalk,
slow steps, leaning on her cane.

There were years when my mother could fill a large room
without a microphone, singing
in three languages.
But this is a time for listening,
for the birds to return her song.

I like to think that birds can recognize
one of their own.
In the late afternoon, they fly to her —
a moorhen, a coot, a summer tanager.
In the distance, a snowy egret
flutters out of the saw grass.
In the coconut trees
a white ibis, a great blue heron.

Turtles gather on the rocks,
swim underwater.
In the saw grass, a purple gallinule
nests on a single egg. The bird lady
points out the green and purple feathers.

That night, my mother dreams about nuclear winter.
The turtles and egrets have disappeared.
Her husband is part of a triumvirate
trying to save the world.

He wants to dance with her
before the ice in the Everglades
freezes the water lilies in the koi pond.

I remember the floods that filled my house
the year the rivers overflowed in Iowa.
It was after the first Persian Gulf War,
and we called it the spring of frogs.
I remember dancing
in a barn surrounded by frogs —
frogs in the trees, frogs in the prairie grass.
Inside the barn Appalachian fiddle music
with frogs patching the red
of the barn board wall.

I never found the entrance
where the frogs came into my house
as rising water rippled the wood
of my bedroom floor.

My mother has always been afraid of frogs.
She closes the screen to keep the geckos outside.

INSIDE A PROFUSION OF BIRDS

My mother talks about dying.
I give her a tangerine shawl
with gold threads,
like your heart, Mama.
She says she wants to be wrapped in it
when she dies. She says
she wants to die on this bed,
and she wants to give me
a small glass clock.

I say, *not yet, Mama.*
Don't be in a hurry. She leans
close to hear what I say.
You have a cold, Mama.
No kisses, only hugs today.
But come close so that
I can feel your heart.

My mother takes too much medicine.
I ask her, what are your
favorite gifts of each day?
Waking up next to my husband.
Doing things with him.
She shows me her favorite picture,
where they are kissing,
and points to the pastel colors
in her bedroom.
Each color is a miracle, she says.

My mother dreams under a pastel comforter
and sleeps long into the morning.
She pads around the house

in teddy bear pajamas
and blue slippers.
While the sun bleeds through a high window,
we eat bagels and whitefish for breakfast.
She walks in her garden, leaning
on a bamboo cane to keep herself standing.
She shows me impatiens,
marigolds, yellow rosebuds.
Each flower is a miracle, she says.

She gives herself small pleasures —
a chocolate raspberry bar,
a ruby-throated hummingbird,
a dogwood tree in the garden.
We listen to Beethoven in the heat,
and I thank her for giving me music.

I tell her about the flowers in California —
calla lilies, birds of paradise,
and my brother's two daughters,
but she won't get on a plane.
The seat is too far from the bathroom, she says.
She tells me about a heron
in the pond around the corner.

I help my Mama zip her dress
over the scars on her back.
I sing to her. We celebrate
her seventy-fifth birthday.
If I live that long,
I want to have long white braids,
song birds flying through my kitchen,
and a body that will carry me.

MAIN STREET IN CEDAR FALLS

You are the cottonwood tree
on the road to Cedar Falls
I forgot to photograph
before it was struck by lightning,
a hawk flying in circles
at the edge of a lavender field.

Maybe it was the cow manure
in the humid air
that late October afternoon
or golden retrievers
running across a plowed
field of alfalfa.

We are standing on a street
where cars don't signal.
You have to watch gestures,
assume they might do anything.

Lacy insects with red wings
fly in through humid
rice paper windows.
When you touch me,
I shiver like a hidden gene.

My hands are ascending notes
on a blue glass bridge
to the memory of a mountain.
My voice is silver, a cumulus cloud
ascending into thunder.

As we dance
a soft light trembles
behind our shoulders,
then travels back home
in a small row of stars.

Autumn is Bare Chested

In the October
morning a maple leaf
on the pavement speaks to me.
Red   Yellow   Wet
It is a sign of something returning.

The rain comes softly.
The rain is an old woman
losing her memory and her speech.
I honor her long white hair.

In the garden
green tomatoes   red chrysanthemums
still blooming
in the growing cold.

At night
the dream of a friend
I don't see anymore.
She is dancing with lacquer fans
in a red kimono.
She is speaking to me again.

The leaves say the move was an obstacle
a hardship to the relationship.
I moved to Iowa.
I can see both sides.

My memories   bare chested
in the garden   in the wind
in the long white rain.

PRAYER

For Lydia and David

A sunny child is playing in the garden.
She sings, smiles to her mother,
chases the cottontail of the rabbit.
Watch her as she runs dancing
between tulips and orange trees.

In the house, a flow of blood,
an angel taking a tiny soul
back to the house of her ancestors
along a trail of shooting stars.

Listen, an invisible voice
is singing to you.
My prayer is that she will return.

For now, turn your eyes
to olive trees, blood red roses,
sunflowers blooming in the garden.
Let the universe hold you in her arms.

GYPSY ROUND

"The clearest way into the universe
is through a forest wilderness."
John Muir

In the birth canal
a waltz in my living room
circles over two rivers
into your kitchen –
the gypsy round.

Sometimes I wonder
if the well of grief is too deep.
Salamanders and swallowtails
in the hollow.

On the night of the full moon
we hike to Cumberland Falls
to see the moonbow.

The voice of the water is silver
like an omen or a bell
as you take my hand and lead me
inside the arch of stone.

High above us the moonbow
arches across the sky.
Tiny droplets of water
fill my body with color and light
where voices are invisible.

My emotions bleed
into the voices of owls

where a small wind
echoes through Cumberland pine
like a banjo.

Something inside me has died.
Whatever is new still pushes
in the birth canal.

Red maple leaves
falling out of the pages
of a book of Chinese paintings.

In the Italian Ghetto

I left a rose on the steps
of the Synagogue in Venice,
then climbed five flights of stairs
to the empty room
where Hebrew voices used to cascade prayers
up to the light that rained through
the Venetian glass dome ceiling —
and hopefully beyond.

Around the room carved benches
and tables where the pious used to study.
Eight scenes from the Exodus painted
in fresco under the windows,
and the words that Moses carried
carved into the walls above
the Ark of the Covenant.
In the center of the room a mosaic
where for centuries
the virgin bride and groom stood
below the wedding canopy.
Above the ark, the eternal light
still burning.

Outside in the *piazza*
rows of apartments stacked too close
on top of one another, the way people lived
for centuries. Italian klezmer music
floats to the street from David's
Judaica shop, a lyric seduction
into an alcove of mirrors
cluttered with silver goblets,

silver candlesticks, woven prayer shawls,
and red Venetian glass.

During the war eight thousand Jews
were deported from Venice.
Only eight returned.
On the wall in the *piazza*
their names and their ages at death
are carved into the wood of a cattle car,
a litany of unfinished lives.

In the distance a bridge of stone
and iron lacework over the water,
lovers wrapped together on wooden seats
of gondolas floating on the Grand Canal.
But the only memory in this room
is bones.

DEJA VU

Pumpkin soup
   with shitake mushrooms.

Chu-chu goes to sleep
   in her new dress.

Something about her presence
   allows me to feel
      my grief.

Eggplants roasting
   on the wood stove
      with sage, owl feather.

In my memory
   the contralto harmony of
      my mother's voice.

Light on the back
   of the head
      of a wooden bird.

TRANSLATION

I follow a trail of light
to the bridge over a koi pond.
The joints hand-crafted with Japanese tools –
old wood, curved, mysterious.
I clap my hands, toss balls of rice
to silver and golden streaming fish
as tiger lilies and irises
sway at the edge of the water.

My mother dreams that she gives me a house –
the one she used to live in.
We put on silk kimonos.
Inside the house, a huge party
singing, a swing band
on the balcony.

By my window
close to the edge of the continent,
I look up the sand dune
to trilliums, ice plant, rosemary
leaning away from the four o'clock
San Francisco wind.

In my own dream I dance
with a man I loved twenty years ago,
spin in his arms to the wisdom
he has gathered since I followed him
through fields of fallow corn and prairie grass.
He has musical hands, made for
improvisation and touching.

In the late afternoon, I play cello —
my passion folded inside the vibrato
the bow a caress
lost inside the music.

In the post office, a Vietnamese man
is singing a monk song.
The melody walks down a mountain
barefoot
in a language I don't understand.

The emotions come from underneath
the muscles,
moving out from the chest
through a forest of bamboo trees
dismantling the shield.

I am almost on the ground
but lifted
through a cadence of summer wind
weaving through prayer flags.

We throw the *I Ching*.
Copper pennies. Old coins.
I don't know how long ago.

His voice is a powder
that tastes like an olive,
a recognition, a stream of light,
as if from under a door.
I listen as my heart
begins
to speak to me again.

WHAT MY FATHER TAUGHT ME

You can't choose the time when a daughter comes to you,
but welcome her into the world with blessings.
Share your toy trains.
Let her build trees of sticks
and lakes of blue paper.
Put her crayon drawings above your drafting table.
Listen to her dreams.

When carpenters leave the roof open,
speak to them in a gentle voice.
Follow your dreams. Even if it takes
eight years of night school.
Bring your daughter to classes on your shoulders.
Buy her a paper doll with a cap and gown.
As you walk across the stage
to get your diploma,
pay attention to her smile.

When the president you campaigned for is assassinated,
take your family to Washington
to put roses on his grave.
Climb the Washington Monument with your daughter,
hand in hand up thousands of stone steps.
Teach her to sacrifice for what she believes.
And if you could do it over,
take her to the March on Washington.

Find your way to be open to the world,
but don't take rides with strangers.
Listen to intuition.
When her hair grows long,
tell her how beautiful she has become.

Learn the language she speaks.
Let her find her wings.

Marriages are better after you are fifty,
but don't do it unless all of the ducks
are pointing in the same direction.
If you've made a mistake, start over.
Find your way to be happy.
Be practical. Don't forget to dream.

FINDING YOU

I dreamed of you in the desert
and in secret tunnels
below the pyramids of Giza.

In initiation chambers
you anointed my feet with jasmine oil
before my journey into the unknown.

You followed me
into the secret passageways
between lives
behind a long row of camels
where I was waiting
for the solstice sun.

I have loved you
inside wide fields of sunflowers,
in the desert with Jupiter rising
over the Eastern mountains,
Cassiopeia floating below
the midheaven,
your hands
light inside a waterfall.

Come to the place where
you can hear the ocean
through the open
skylight.

Carry the moon.
Bring your hands of silver.

If you were here,
we'd be touching.

MASK AWAKENING EGYPTIAN DREAM

> The Sufis explain that the union
> of the animal and the angel
> makes a full human being.
>   Alzak Amlani

1.   Mask

Khnum
Ram-Headed God of Creation
forming human figures like clay
on a potter's wheel.

Animal head, human body
awkward transition at the river
where the ram's neck
curves into the human.

Sandstone, traces of paint
cobalt inside the shimmering
desert heat.

Creator of the Ankh
ancient sign of life
the long base still visible
between
his thumb and fingers.

You are the priest
with the leopard skin
around your back,
the tail a painted passageway,
light and shadow
curving to the underworld.

2.   Stela

The women gather roots and powders
grind indigo, red berries,
copper salts, alum, madder root,
walnut pods, wild chamomile,
pomegranate skins,
black mordant, wild mustard.

The priest beside the Lion
of Amenhotep
visits the temple dancer,
carves Hathor with his lover's face
and cow's ears.

He writes his dreams in hieroglyphs
on the walls of Pharoah's tomb
using reeds with pointed ends,
mixes powders with Nile water,
ochre, red and cobalt.

He paints the stela for his mother –
flying gazelles, dancing turtles, river mud,
drawings from the *Egyptian
Book of the Dead.*

3.   Dream

Before the moon rises,
the women weave reeds
from the green banks of the Nile.
They prepare to dream
where the animal meets the human.

A turtle protects his head
inside the King's Chamber,
where shafts of light
open his vision to the other world.

He sleeps on a carved headrest
in the shape of a gazelle
holding a hieroglyph.

He dreams of cobalt stars
a long legged, long-eared creature
without a name.
He sings the way light slides down
the side of a pyramid.

A sandstone lion is the guardian.
He faces all directions.
Beyond that, a flood of starlight –
Isis holding a copper moon
over her head.

In the morning, a vision
of Amun-Re, the Sun God
you have become.

4.   Awakening

If you look at Egyptian art,
you can see what their dreams were like...

King, God, flying turtle
monkey riding a horse
crocodile head, truth feather, hippopotamus
bottle in the form of a lute
a blue-armed woman plays.

Royal women carved alabaster.
Common women painted,
carved in wood.
In the gods
a shimmering in the neck
where the animal meets the human.

In the place of initiation,
you sing inside the pyramids...

Eye of the Sphinx, turquoise beetle
striped fish spawning on a river
blue glass amulet.
Young woman holding a copper box on her head
nude except for her headband
and gold bracelets.

If you sing for five thousand years,
you will see her in your dreams.

About the Author

Diane Frank is an award winning poet. Her friends describe her as a harem of seven women in one very small body. She has mentored hundreds of writers at San Francisco State University, City College of San Francisco, The University of Vermont, and the Professional Writing Program at MIU in Fairfield, Iowa. Currently, she lives in San Francisco – where she dances, plays cello, teaches writing workshops, and creates her life as an art form. She is also a documentary scriptwriter with expertise in Eastern and sacred art. *Blackberries in the Dream House*, her first novel, was nominated for the Pulitzer Prize.

Website: www.dianefrank.net
E-mail: GeishaPoet@aol.com.

ABOUT THE ARTISTS

Philip Sugden is best known for his exquisite drawings of Tibet and the Himalayas. He studied under the French painter, Arnaud D'Hauterives, in Paris. Since graduation from the New York School of Visual Arts and the Paris American Academie des Beaux Arts, he has made eleven journeys throughout the Himalayas and Tibet. With his partner, Carole Elchert, he created a PBS television show and a companion book titled, *White Lotus, An Introduction to Tibetan Culture*, published by Snow Lion. They also hosted the Dalai Lama's speaking engagement at The University of Findlay, where both are faculty in Fine Arts. His drawings are published in an exquisite full-color book titled, *Visions from the Fields of Merit: Drawings of Tibet and the Himalayas*, published by Floating Temple Press. Philip is part of the Fine Arts faculty at Bluffton University.

Melanie Gendron is a celebrated visionary artist, author and poet. Her art embodies her reverence for nature, her love of the human figure, and mythological symbols in the shaman tradition of her Native American background. She studied painting, sculpture and writing at The Boston Museum School of Art in affiliation with Tufts University. She is also skilled in fashion design, photography, computer graphics, multimedia communications and digital painting. Melanie created The Gendron Tarot deck of visionary art, with a companion book, published by U.S. Games Systems, Inc. She also designs books with original illustrations and covers for Blue Light Press and other publications. She lives and works in the Santa Cruz mountains of California. Her website is www.melaniegendron.com.

OTHER BOOKS BY DIANE FRANK

Blackberries in the Dream House
(1ˢᵗ World Library: Austin - Delhi - Fairfield, Iowa, 2003).

The Winter Life of Shooting Stars
(Blue Light Press: Fairfield, Iowa, 1999).

The All Night Yemenite Café
(Dark River Press: Davenport, Iowa, 1993).

Rhododendron Shedding Its Skin
(Blue Light Press: San Francisco, California, 1988).

Isis: Poems by Diane Frank
(Project Press: Los Angeles, California, 1982).

ANTHOLOGY PUBLICATIONS

River of Earth and Sky: Poems for the Twenty-First Century
(Blue Light Press - 1ˢᵗ World Library:
Austin - Delhi - Fairfield, Iowa, 2006).

The Dryland Fish: An Anthology of Contemporary Iowa Poets
(1ˢᵗ World Library: Fairfield, Iowa, 2003).

Eclipsed Moon Coins: Twenty-Six Visionary Poets
(Blue Light Press: Fairfield, Iowa, 1997).

Voices on the Landscape: Contemporary Iowa Poets
(Loess Hills Press: Iowa, 1996).

The Book of Eros: Arts and Letters from Yellow Silk
(Harmony Books: New York, 1995).

Printed in the United States

CPSIA information can be obtained
at www.ICGtesting.com
Printed in the USA
BVHW071419180419
545903BV00002B/136/P